Dedication

This book is dedicated to all business owners.

Acknowledgements

First and foremost, I thank God for guiding me in all that I do. It is by His grace that I am able to accomplish anything in this life.

I would like to express my deepest gratitude to Lissa Woodson for her expertise and developmental input. She is the oil that encourages my writing motor to keep running when it threatens to sputter to a halt. Thank you to bestselling author, Naleighna Kai, for her input; my editorial team, led by Katie Walsh; my readers, Lois Eichacker, Trina Streeter-Kluka, Pamela Meekins, William Meekins and Shaquela Tracy; and David Sokol for the beautiful cover design. Much appreciation to Ehryck F. Gilmore, CH, for your continued insight as the world's best life coach and for promoting my books as if they were your own; Tim Newlin for the wonderful interior artwork; and Mark Daniels for taking my company's technology to the next level.

I would also like to thank Natalie Chadwell, Belinda Turner and Kimauna Catchings for going well beyond the call of duty by arranging the book signing for my first book, 'The Naked Truth of Owning a Business', and encouraging and supporting me; and my sister, Carole Meekins, for her unwavering support and for being an exceptional unpaid book promoter.

I acknowledge Sheila Bonner, Sheila Boyd, Kelly Gilbert, Darren McKinnis, Clarence Montgomery, Paula Ross and Astrid Tompkins for their inspiration and support. Last but not least, I would like to thank my husband, Byron Powers, for being the most dependable person in my life and supporting me in everything that I do.

And to the new business owner reading this book, I wish you much success with your new venture, and may you find something within these pages that helps you realize your dream of running a successful business.

"Whenever you see a successful business, someone once made a courageous decision."

--Peter F. Drucker – Author & Consultant

About This Book

This book is for those of you who have decided that you're ready to launch a business but still have some unanswered questions and concerns. In my book, 'The Naked Truth of Owning a Business' (Shameless Plug #1), I shared personal traits and lifestyle issues that should be taken into consideration before deciding to open a business. If you have not already done so, now might be a good time to read that book.

In this book, we've moved past the yellow brick road of deciding whether or not we are cut out for business ownership to actually reaching Oz and planning the launch. I will answer common questions and highlight actual cases to help you learn from the successes of others and keep you from making their same mistakes. Please note that no individual business owner is represented in any of the cases. They are composites of situations that actually occurred but have been altered to protect those who may have run into a wicked witch or two on their journey to Oz. If one or two of the cases seem similar to your personal experiences, find comfort in the knowledge that you are not alone.

Before we start, I apologize in advance if I "hit a nerve" with some of my discussions and cases. I prefer to get right to the point without a lot of 'political correctness'. The truth is the truth, and in the end it will help you (if you choose to listen).

Next, whenever possible I will refer you to other informational sources, instead of reinventing the wheel. There's no point in me repeating something that is better stated elsewhere.

Third, this book is short and to the point, so you can get through it in a few hours or less. Being a business owner myself, I know you don't have a lot of time to dedicate to reading unnecessary verbiage.

Fourth, it is intended to be easily understood by everyone so it is not loaded with technical jargon, which means you won't need a reference manual or an interpreter to understand the concepts presented within these pages. In fact, my five-year-old Goddaughter read it in several hours and has launched a lemonade stand franchise. Just kidding!

Finally, this book is not based on detailed studies and statistics. Even I find it boring to read pages and pages of tables and statistics, and I'm an accountant! I didn't hold a bunch of people hostage in focus groups like McDonald's does when testing out their latest sandwich, nor did I send out questionnaires. This book is based on my observations over the last twenty years of working and interacting with business owners.

If you are reading this book, you probably fit into one of three categories: a) you are a friend of mine and are supporting me based solely on the fact that you know me, b) you are a relative and are reading it because we share bloodlines, or c) you have actually decided to launch a business. I choose to believe that you fall into the last category.

Hopefully, you have indulged your passion for the business idea that has been burning inside of you like a five-alarm bowl of Texas chili. By that I mean that you've at least written a business plan, concluded that the idea is solid, and determined that you have what it takes to run a business. Your family is supportive of your decision, and you have the financial and human resources available to execute your strategy. You've put on your gym shoes, jogged down the entrepreneurial yellow brick road and have finally made it to the mysterious hall of the great Oz, and you're asking, "Now what?"

"Run your business like a business and it will be more successful."

Should I Incorporate?

One of the most common questions from prospective entrepreneurs is, "Should I incorporate?" In most cases, my answer is a resounding, "Yes." I believe that if there is any possibility that someone might sue you for the products or services your business provides, you should incorporate. We live in a very litigious society, and people have sued for things that seem too ridiculous to be real – for example, a suit against a haunted house for being too scary, or one against a beer company that falsely advertised that women would come to life whenever someone drank their beer. True, both the haunted house and beer ad campaign lawsuits were thrown out, but I include them to reinforce the point that there may be a lawsuit lurking just outside your door. You don't want to be that business owner who loses their house, personal savings and trophy spouse because you were too cheap to hire a good attorney to incorporate your business and didn't purchase adequate insurance.

The next question I am frequently asked is, "Should my business be a traditional Corporation (commonly referred to as a C-Corp), S-Corporation, Partnership, Limited Liability Company, etc.? My answer is always, "It depends."

Due to the importance of this topic, I have included the definitions of the most common types of business structures in the Appendix. The important stuff always tends to be a bit boring, but it's important, so I'm giving you the choice. Either grab a cup of coffee or a sugary soft drink and try to stay awake while you read the few paragraphs on Pages 114 through 117 in the Appendix or keep going and read it when you get to the end.

According to the Internal Revenue Service (IRS), "the most common forms of business are the Sole Proprietorship, Partnership, Corporation, and S Corporation." The Limited Liability Company (LLC) is a relatively new business structure that is becoming more and more popular. In my experience, a significant number of new small-business owners elect to be structured as S Corporations or LLCs. Keep in mind that the business structure that you select should be driven by legal and tax considerations, your end goal for your business, whether or not you intend to have partners, what is typical in your industry, among others. Here are some things to consider:

- If your goal is to establish a business that you can sell at some point in the near future then an attorney should structure your business to make it easier and less costly to consummate a sale.

- If your success will be dependent on numerous joint ventures with different partners then perhaps an LLC is the best structure for you.

- If you are on your third marriage and are still annoyed that your ex got the last business in the divorce settlement, you might want to make sure that you understand the ramifications of a divorce on the business structure you select.

- If you don't want to be burdened by the corporate requirements of an annual meeting, minutes, etc., you will probably be advised to consider an LLC.

The intent of this chapter is not to give you the answer and tell you the type of structure you should choose. Instead, it is to point out that the decision is based on many variables that you need to consider before making a decision. There are numerous resources available about business structures, and each may lead you to a different conclusion. A good resource that clearly spells out the differences can be found on the Internal Revenue Service website at http://www.irs.gov/businesses/small/article/0,,id=98359,00.html.

There may also be useful information on your state website. Keep in mind that when you incorporate, you will be required to file corporate income and payroll tax returns, file annual reports with your state, obtain appropriate business licenses, conduct and document board meetings and maintain appropriate corporate records and documents.

Once you've completed the initial research, and you're armed with a basic understanding of the differences between the structures, you should meet with an experienced attorney or certified public accountant (and no, that wasn't a shameless plug). They will (or should) ask you a host of questions before they make a recommendation.

Some of the questions you may want to consider are:

- Will your business have enough risk to require a corporate structure or will adequate insurance be sufficient?

- Will you be able to keep up with the extra paperwork required by a corporation?

- Will you need the tax advantages of certain business structures when you start out?

- What business structure is typical in the industry?

- Will you have partners, and if so, how many?

- Do you intend to leave this business to your children as a legacy, or are you building the business for sale in the future?

- Do you have any other businesses?

- What is your personal net worth?

- Have you done estate planning?

- Will you be employed by the business, and do you expect to retire from it?

- Do you need benefits, such as health insurance?

- Do you expect your business to be profitable from day one?

There are many more questions, but these are just some of the ones that I feel you should be prepared to answer. If you are muttering to yourself that you went to an attorney who quoted what you feel is an arm and a leg with a couple of toes thrown in just to incorporate your business, understand that the business structure you select is very important and should not be taken lightly. It could cost you more in the long run if you omit some important documents when you organize your business. You should not have to sell your first born to pay for it, but you should be prepared to pay a reasonable fee to get it done right!

Another important step in establishing your business is to

meet with an insurance broker to ensure that you have the proper types and amounts of insurance coverage for your business. Take a look at the following case study to see why this is so critical.

CASE STUDY 1:

Callie and her sons operate a landscaping business. It started off with mowing and maintaining the lawns of their friends and neighbors. As time went on, more clients came their way. They decided that they needed to hire more workers to keep up with the workload and put an ad on Craigslist. After interviewing several candidates, they ended up hiring Carlos and Mike.

Things went well for several months and Callie was thrilled with the increase in business. One day while Carlos and Mike were trimming a customer's shrubs, Carlos tripped over a cord and ended up cutting Mike's right hand instead of the bush. Although he immediately rushed Mike to the hospital, they were unable to save the three middle fingers on Mike's right hand. Since Mike was right-handed, he could no longer work as a landscaper. When he inquired about workers compensation benefits, he soon learned that Callie and Sons had failed to purchase it. He initiated a lawsuit, and the process became a hard lesson for Callie.

Not only had she failed to purchase workers' compensation insurance, but she had not purchased any business liability insurance and had never incorporated the business. As the lawsuit progressed, her business, dream home and savings were at risk—all from one unforeseen incident.

The above case is a sad example of what can happen if you don't protect your personal assets by incorporating and purchasing the appropriate amount of business insurance.

"Becoming wealthy is not a matter of how much you earn, who your parents are, or what you do ... it is a matter of managing your money properly. "

--Noel Whittaker -- Investment planner, public speaker, personal finance writer.

Don't Pay Your Personal Bills
out of the Business Account

Nothing personal, it's just business. Personal and Business are two separate words, and if you keep that in mind, you'll stay out of trouble. Your business is a separate entity from you, and therefore the business checking account should not be treated like your personal slush fund. Just because you own the business, doesn't mean that you should have your alimony, child support, credit card payments, and vacation expenses automatically deducted from the business checking account. Tapping into your business like it's an ATM can turn into an accounting nightmare, which works for CPAs like me because it may increase our fees. Keep in mind that you'll need to maintain adequate documentation supporting the business purpose of the withdrawals, or you could have big problems with three little letters...IRS.

When I refer to using your business account for personal purposes, I'm not talking about the occasional slip up where you accidently pull the wrong debit card out of your wallet while making a purchase. Everyone is allowed a mistake or two. I am also not referring to distributions taken by partners or members of an LLC. I'm talking about routinely paying the baby sitter, the hair stylist and your favorite restaurant by writing a check or withdrawing cash from the business account. You know you better than you know anyone else. If you won't have the financial discipline to keep the business debit card in your wallet when you're at a romantic dinner, trying to impress your latest love interest, then don't have the bank give you a debit card for your business checking account. Your accountant does not want to routinely see card transactions for nail and hair salons, toy stores or clothing stores, which are generally not valid business expenses.

According to the Internal Revenue Service, to be tax deductible, a business expense must be both ordinary and necessary. An ordinary expense is one that is common and accepted in your trade or business. A necessary expense is one that is helpful and appropriate for your industry. Your friend may be able to deduct certain items for their business that are not deductible for you. For example, a therapy company that uses a dog for therapeutic purposes may be able to deduct pet food as a business expense. As a CPA, I cannot deduct the food that I purchase for my dogs. As cute as Bailey (my Yorkshire Terrier/Maltese mix) is, I don't think my clients would appreciate my bringing him to their appointments in an attempt to calm them down when they learn how much they owe in taxes! It would be a nice try, but…no!

When you think about what a valid business expense is, think of it as something you would be reimbursed for if you did not own the company. For example, if you worked at IBM and purchased a new television set for your family room, would you be able to claim that purchase on your employee expense reimbursement form? NOT!

Also, don't confuse your personal wardrobe with a uniform. Of course a uniform that you purchase for your business is a valid expense and deductible on the business tax return. However, that new pair of designer stilettos that you just had to have for a New Year's Eve party but realized that your personal account wouldn't stretch to cover…no that doesn't cut it as a business expense.

However, if you're employed in one of the salacious bordellos in Nevada, you might have a fighting chance.

When you incorporate, you are creating a legal entity separate and distinct from yourself, and the assets of that entity are not there for you to just take and use for whatever you want. IRS Publication 535 is an excellent resource for learning about tax deductible business expenses and can be downloaded from http://www.irs.gov/publications/p535/index.html

There are legal reasons why you shouldn't use your business checkbook to pay your personal expenses. I am not an attorney and will therefore refer you to your attorney for details about the concept of "piercing the corporate veil' and how it may apply to your particular company. However, I know enough about it to highlight the basics for you in layman's terms.

One of the main reasons for incorporating is to protect your personal assets from the debts and activities of the company. However, there are situations when you, as a business owner, can be considered accountable for actions conducted by your corporation. If, for some unfortunate reason, you are sued, a court can "pierce" your corporate "veil" and hold you responsible for actions taken by your corporation against other corporations and individuals as well as certain business debts. If you are sued, an astute attorney could try to pierce your company's veil for any of the following:

- Commingling your personal funds with your business funds by paying personal bills out of your corporate account.
- Failing to file and maintain the appropriate incorporating documents and filings (e.g. minutes of board of director's meetings).
- Using your personal name instead of the corporate name

when conducting business and executing contracts.

• Playing solitaire on your business computer during business hours (Aha! Caught you sleeping. Just kidding.)

If an attorney can prove that you are using the corporation personally, they may be able to "pierce the corporate veil" and at that point, your personal assets may no longer be protected. Again, I reiterate that I am NOT an attorney, and you should contact an attorney if you are worried about this issue or are facing a potential lawsuit. It should be noted that in many business transactions, you, as the business owner, are required to provide a personal guarantee. In those situations you are responsible for the debt regardless of whether or not your business is incorporated.

CASE STUDY 2:

Darnell was viewed as a mover and shaker by many of his friends because he carried a 14-karat gold money clip full of cash (lots of singles in the middle of a few twenty dollar bills) and was always running around "doing business." Darnell was incessantly on the telephone barking orders to his many independent contractors. What everyone didn't know was that over the years, he had received enough threatening letters from the IRS to wallpaper a bedroom. He had gone through a string of accountants, looking for the cheapest one to fix his problems. Darnell ran from the ones who quoted him a price he didn't want to pay and eagerly turned over the IRS correspondence to the ones who said they would "fix him up" for cash. After each one fixed him up, he was out a couple of hundred dollars and continued to receive letters from the IRS.

He finally decided to work with a CPA who was referred to him by another business owner. After reviewing Darnell's documentation, the new CPA quickly realized that Darnell had been using his company like his personal bank account. He was paying cash to his independent contractors because they had requested cash – and preparing 1099s for them had never crossed his mind. He deposited and withdrew large sums of cash to and from the company bank account on an almost daily basis and failed to retain supporting documentation for any of the transactions. To add insult to injury, he had neglected to file his business income tax returns for four years. He had also been kicked off the tax filing and reporting services of the payroll processing service he was using several years earlier because his payroll kept bouncing when the service attempted to withdraw the tax payments from his bank account. When the tax service kicked him off, they forwarded the quarterly payroll tax returns for him to file. He didn't even open the envelopes! He now owed payroll taxes, income taxes, sizeable penalties and interest charges.

Over time, his new CPA resolved all of his issues, and Darnell opened a personal bank account. He is now genuinely trying to reconstruct that corporate veil that he had been tearing to shreds for many years.

Once you incorporate your business, make sure that you:

- Use business checking accounts and credit cards exclusively for business purposes.
- Pay yourself in a manner consistent with your business structure and in accordance with your CPA's or attorney's advice (e.g. distributions versus salary).

- Retain all receipts in an organized manner.

- Conduct and document your shareholder/partnership/board of director meetings.

- File your annual filings with the state. For example, in the state of Illinois, you are required to file an annual report with the Secretary of State to prevent involuntary dissolution of your corporation.

- Use expense reimbursement forms or some other mechanism to document business expenses that you pay for out of pocket. (The big boys don't make you fill out expense reimbursement forms because they like paper.) Don't just write yourself a check!

- File your business taxes in a timely manner!!!

- Consider a reputable payroll-processing company to ensure that your payroll taxes are deposited and all payroll forms are prepared in a timely and accurate manner.

- PURCHASE BUSINESS INSURANCE!

The main point I want you to take away from this chapter is: treat your company separately and distinctly from you, the individual, and you should not have any problems. Owning a corporation is serious business, regardless of its structure and size. If you start off right when it's small, you will (hopefully) develop the discipline and practices necessary to stay out of trouble as your business grows.

timtim.com

"Entrepreneurs are risk takers, willing to roll the dice with their money or reputation on the line in support of an idea or enterprise. They willingly assume responsibility for the success or failure of a venture and are answerable for all its facets."

--Victor Kiam
Entrepreneur & Owner of New England Patriots

You Don't Get Paid if I Don't Get Paid

During my twenty-plus years as a CPA, I have continued to hear horror stories about small business owners getting into trouble by paying themselves too much too soon and failing to reinvest in their businesses. It's important for business owners to be aware of the fact that they should be the last ones paid. Okay, let me say that a second time. BUSINESS OWNERS SHOULD BE THE LAST ONES PAID. Now, let me get down off my soapbox and give it to you straight, no chaser: I don't care if you are working so hard that you feel as though you are rebuilding the Great Pyramids! Owners are paid last. Your employees and vendors are not responsible for the business risk that you took. You decided to start a business; they decided to work for you with every intention of getting a paycheck. They are your employees because they didn't want to or plan on taking that risk. If that were the case, they would be reading my first book and starting their OWN businesses. And your vendors expect and deserve to be paid. After all, they did provide a service to you to keep your business running!

Just because you are a small business, does not give you the right to call your workers into the conference room and profess, "We are short on cash this pay period, so you don't get paid if I don't get paid." In all honesty, your employees don't care if you don't get paid. And if you want to know the truth, they assume that you get paid a whole lot more than they do and should have saved something for a rainy day (or at least have an umbrella handy so that they don't get wet). This situation brings to mind an old saying: don't urinate (the real word starts with a p and ended with an s) on me and tell me it's raining. There is nothing more comical than a business owner who is driving a top-of-the-line Mercedes, living in a nice 5,000-square-foot home, and then not being able to meet their payroll.

CASE STUDY 3:

Felicia is the sole owner of a multi-million dollar business. She has an outgoing personality and markets her business every opportunity she gets. However, she has no financial discipline. She wears only the best designer suits and leases a new eighty thousand dollar Mercedes every three years. She pays herself a high six-figure salary and has no savings or retirement plan.

From time to time, Felicia's business experiences cash-flow problems. During those times, her lack of personal wealth and mediocre credit score prevent her from securing a line of credit for her business. Therefore, she is forced to rely on family employees and her management team deferring their paychecks, so she can pay front-line staff. Her family accepts the situation because they know their pay is excessive relative to their skills and education. The management team agrees to help out because they, unlike her, have sufficient personal savings, allowing them to defer their paychecks and still meet their financial obligations.

As the years passed, the members of the management team moved on to other professional endeavors, and Felicia did not save any of the funds generated by the resulting decrease in payroll. Therefore, when she hit that financial brick wall, and there were no management team salaries to defer, she was unable to pay any of her staff.

During the most recent cash crunch, Felicia called all of her staff into the conference room and told them that they were not going to be paid. Her exact words were "If I don't get paid, then you don't get paid." The staff was stunned at her lack of concern for their well-being. Felicia's line of business depended heavily on front-line staff, a fact that she failed to take into consideration during her announcement.

Sure enough, several of her most experienced front-line staff members resigned and went to work for a competitor. Not only did she lose crucial employees, but her cash flow issues were now being openly discussed by her employees, customers and business associates.

Felicia made several mistakes. First and foremost, she lacked financial discipline. She failed to accept the fact that it was up to her to make up the cash shortfall to meet payroll. The better way to approach her business would have been to adopt a savings plan and set aside cash reserves for her business, instead of spending lavishly on herself and her family.

Second, she should have been more sensitive to the sacrifices her employees were making by not getting paid in a timely manner. Making statements to your employees regarding your pay is inappropriate, in poor taste and should never be uttered by a business owner. Felicia's employees would have been more appreciative of a sympathetic approach that thanked them for their shared sacrifice, then hit them with the bad news. A few of them still might have flipped to a competitor, but it is far less likely that her business would be "out in the street" in a way that could affect her company in the long-term. Paychecks are one thing, but a big, in your face, "up yours" is something people don't brush off with a simple, "Well, she's in the same boat we are."

Finally, if you lead an ostentatious lifestyle then you need to either make sure that you have cash reserves or that your employees don't know that you are living large. Employees are watching you and your spending habits. They want to be confident that everything is under control and on the up and up. When you start missing payrolls, they will wonder why you just purchased that new floor-length fur coat or why you just took that seven day trip to the Bahamas. Ultimately, when your staff loses confidence in your decision-making ability and your ability to understand their need to get a paycheck while you're sliding your well-paid buttocks behind the wheel of that Mercedes, they will leave. And as we all know (or should know if you are starting a business), it is very costly to hire and train new staff.

Never lose sight of the fact that you can start the business, but you need a solid workforce to keep it. When you launch your business remember that, at first, you may not make more money than your employees. Highly capable employees demand near market salaries and you may have to take a little out of your pocket to ensure that you have the best staff possible. Remember one valuable thing: YOU are the only person willing to work for your company for free. When you get a good staff, don't take them for granted. It's difficult to retain honest, ethical, skilled and loyal employees. When you have them, do everything in your power to keep them.

There will be times when your cash flow is challenged, but if you set aside funds when times are good, you will be better able to survive the more difficult times. That luxury car, fur coat and designer suit that you purchased will not help you when your customers are late paying you and you have a payroll to meet. Put it in the bank! When you have enough set aside, then splurge on yourself.

"It is rare to find a business partner who is selfless. If you are lucky it happens once in a lifetime."

--Michael Eisner – Businessman, Past CEO of Walt Disney

Is There Safety in Numbers?

I am not an advocate of partnering for the sake of partnering. Just because you and Cousin Bob both want to be business owners, does not mean that you should dive headfirst into the deep end of the pool and form a venture together. In my book, 'The Naked Truth of Owning a Business', (Shameless Plug #2), I addressed the potential pitfalls of taking on a partner. In fact, I named that particular chapter "Partnership or Prisoner?" There are many ways you can work with other parties without legally marrying them. Sometimes joint ownership, if the parties don't share the same goals, ethics and degree of financial discipline, can be downright disastrous. Safety in numbers isn't the dynamic that works when you operate with a poorly thought out and undocumented partnership.

CASE STUDY 4:

Alexa and John had been married for thirty years and were successful entrepreneurs. In their late fifties, they decided to open a home-health agency. At that time, many home-health agencies were being opened in the state, and it appeared to be a profitable industry. They recruited Tammy, a close family friend, who was an experienced registered nurse to work with them. John had a lot of contacts and potential referral sources, so they weren't concerned about their ability to attract and retain a steady customer base.

While they were in the planning stages of the business, John remembered that an acquaintance had worked for many years in a home-care agency. He thought he remembered that José was also a nurse practitioner and was married to Maria, a physical therapist. John suggested that José and Maria also join in on the venture and contribute their knowledge and expertise to the business, while he and Alexa contributed the startup capital.

When José convinced them that his cousin, Valdez, a medical billing expert, would add significant value, they brought him on and suddenly had six shareholders. John was an honest and trusting soul who thought nothing was amiss when José suggested that he, his wife and cousin own 51 percent of the shares, since they would be handling the daily operations of the company.

John was an astute businessman and had an attorney draw up a detailed shareholder agreement. Everyone agreed that they would not compensate themselves until it was determined that the business was on solid financial footing.

In the beginning, everything worked well. They completed all the tasks necessary to become licensed and accredited and opened their doors. Due to John's connections, they were flooded with patient referrals, and it looked as though the business would be profitable very quickly.

Then, the money started rolling in, and the truth started ooz-ing out. They found out that José was not really a nurse practitio-ner, and Valdez had no experience in home-health billing. Maria refused to provide nursing care to their patients without a paycheck, even though they had all agreed to defer compensation. José also had an explosive temper, which scared the other partners and em-ployees alike. The money kept rolling in, but the partners were fight-ing like Ali and Frazier! Alexa, John, and Tammy felt that the other three owners were not providing quality service and suggested that they sell their shares. When they refused, an all-out war began.

First, Alexa, John, and Tammy (Group A) locked José, Maria and Valdez (Group B) out of the office. Group B hired an attorney to file the paperwork necessary to gain access to the business and then promptly locked Group A out. Group A changed the remittance address and bank account so that Group B no longer had access to the funds. Group B changed it back, and so on.

Group A and B became locked in a messy lawsuit to de-termine which parties would buy out the others and at what price. Group B would rather close the business, than give it to Group A. Although there was a shareholder agreement, it had never been signed; therefore state law dictated the terms under which the par-ties could dissolve the company. In this particular state, at least four of the six partners' votes were needed to accomplish that regret-ful task. Unfortunately, with three people in each group, neither side had a leg to stand on.

Today, legal motions and summons are flying back and forth, and the only ones making money are the attorneys.

In the case above, there were many more circumstances that led to the decision to split up. There are not enough pages in this book to document all the things that went wrong (especially since I promised to keep it short). However, even though the parties launched a successful business, it very quickly began to fall apart because the parties did not do their due diligence (research) before starting a business together. Credit checks? No. Background checks? No. Even something as simple as having each person provide business references and calling those references would have sent up red flags. On the business tip, they also failed to execute their shareholder agreement. People who initially respected each other became the home-health-care field's version of the Hatfields and the McCoys.

Be very careful when you are considering joint business ownership – Points to ponder:

- Don't rush into it. It may be just as difficult to get out of a bad business partnership as it is to get out of a bad marriage. The novelty or newness of the partnership can fade fast, and that's when the trouble begins.

- Keep in mind that everyone who adds value to your business does not need to be a partner, member or a shareholder. In the case above, Alexa, John and Tammy could have simply hired or contracted with the other three parties or found other, more qualified employees to perform the billing and administrative functions they were entrusting to José and Valdez.

- Don't give away control of your business. It may not be possible to retain control if you are relying on someone else's money to get your venture off the ground but try your hardest.

- Hire a reputable attorney to put the details of your agreement in writing before the money starts to roll in. Have a partnership/ shareholder/operating agreement prepared that outlines how the venture will operate and the circumstances under which the parties can exit or dissolve the business. And make sure that everyone signs the agreement!

If you are seriously considering partnering with a friend, associate, family member, dog or cat…DOCUMENT, DOCUMENT, DOCUMENT!!! And do your due diligence. The following are a few questions to think about before you take the leap with another party:

- Have you and your potential partner shared your credit reports? Will your prospective partner's credit score benefit or hinder your ability to secure credit? If your partner has a poor credit score, are you prepared to be the one signing on the dotted line for the personal guarantees and debt?

- Do both of you intend to quit your day jobs? If

so, are you both able to delay compensation?

- Will one of you be contributing more sweat equity (time and energy versus cash) than the other? If so, how do you plan to account for this difference?

- Have you verified the credentials and/ or licenses of your prospective business partner(s)? (Large corporations routinely verify credentials, but often associates who plan to start a business together miss this important step.)

- Is your prospective partner truly qualified to perform their assigned functions (e.g. your bookkeeper partner acting as CFO)?

- Is there a need to obtain criminal background checks, (e.g. in businesses working with children) and will you and your partner pass?

- What will happen if one of you dies? Are you prepared to work with your partner's husband, children or Cousin Bob?

- What is your motivation for partnering? Do you really need their expertise or capital or are you just afraid? Why not consider collaborating or a loan instead?

I could go on and on about the need to be cautious when going into business with another party. I have seen and heard of so many horror stories that occurred simply because neither party did their homework. The worst cases are where there is not a fully executed operating/partnership/shareholder agreement.

Poorly planned business partnerships are similar to marrying someone you barely know, only to later find out that your new spouse is the custodial parent to five young children, has had three marriages before yours and doesn't have two nickels to rub together. It's not that I don't like children or disapprove of multiple marriages, but this is information that you really needed to know before you purchased your big, white ball gown or Armani tuxedo and strutted down the aisle.

Tim Nardin

"Like car accidents, most hardware problems are due to driver error." --Unknown

I Have a Perfectly Good Computer at Home

One of my close business associates runs a technology company, and the horror stories around technology and small businesses bear repeating. Since you have decided to start a business, two of the first things you will need to do is to create a detailed budget and to secure/save/beg for sufficient startup capital. Technology needs (both hardware and software) should be a part of that budget. Reliable technology is an integral part of a successful business venture; you must have computers that work, regular backups, disaster recovery plans, etc. Oh, and let's not forget about purchasing valid software licenses.

If you lose all of your data while running a business, you will have just created a brand spanking new data entry job for some unsuspecting soul. Including technology in your budget is not about having ten brand new shiny top-of-the-line computers, printers and a server that you can't afford. I am suggesting that you develop a budget and work with a qualified technology consultant to determine the most cost-effective way for you to acquire the amount of technology necessary to get you started. Open box sales, refurbished equipment and good used equipment reign supreme on the internet. However, make sure that a knowledgeable technology professional consults with you about your equipment needs and planned purchases. Don't learn the hard way.

When I started my accounting firm, I had two five-year-old computers. I maintained one for personal use and the other exclusively for business. On the business computer, I did not store pictures, music or any non-business related information. Also, I didn't allow anyone else to access that computer, since it contained sensitive information about my customers. I kept the virus protection up-to-date and maintained backups of key files. My old business computer served me well for a few years. However, when I hired a staff person who needed to access information simultaneously, I had to invest in some sort of network. Even though the accountant in me wanted to take the inexpensive way out, I knew that the business was growing and took the recommendation of my technologically savvy friends and purchased equipment and a bunch of software that I couldn't name or spell. My friends tried their hardest to explain the purpose for all the equipment and software to me, but my eyes glazed over at every attempt. I must admit that it was like trying to teach my ten-year-old Doberman to play nice with my Morkie. He just doesn't get it, and neither did I. But the one thing I can say is that I forgot all about the confusion the minute the equipment was installed and running smoothly.

CASE STUDY 5:

Walter owns a $10 million health-care company. He purchased a state-of-the-art clinical management system, but acquired his accounting software from Paul, his discount technology consul-

tant, for a fraction of what the vendor would have charged. One day while his fifteen-dollar-an-hour bookkeeper was entering data into his accounting system, she received a message that the system would be locked until the program was registered. Walter called Paul, seeking his assistance with the matter. When he didn't receive a call back after several hours, he decided to register the program himself, since his bookkeeper was on the clock.

When he called the software vendor, he was advised that his license number was already registered to another business. He frantically called Paul again and again to no avail. Paul had disappeared! Walter ended up purchasing a full-price system from the vendor so he could access his accounting data, and he had to pay the bookkeeper for the time she sat while he resolved the issue.

When I budgeted for my network purchase, I was horrified to learn that I needed annual licenses which cost almost as much as the hardware itself (a little exaggeration, but you get the point). While that was a bit of a shock, I preferred that everything about my business be legitimate. You can't claim to be an ethical company or that you're doing God's will by starting a business if you are buying "bootleg" software, which is synonymous with stealing. In the case above, Walter thought he was getting a great deal by purchasing software for an unreasonably cheap price. Unfortunately, he didn't bother to verify that the software was licensed to his company. Bottom line? If your company can afford to be in business, you can afford to purchase valid software. If you want to scrimp, do it with company-paid lunches, golf outings, or your own salary, not with your software. It may end up costing you much more than you saved.

If someone tells you that they can "hook you up" for what seems like an unreasonable price, beware!

Case Study 6:

Sarah started a bookkeeping business in her home office. She was successful from the very beginning and had been very frugal when it came to spending money on startup costs. She used a seven-year-old computer that served her well. She maintained four years of accounting software, as well as multiple tax programs on this computer. However, her thirteen-year-old son also used the computer for doing homework, sending emails, surfing the internet, downloading music and social networking.

Every six weeks or so she would complain to Paul, her friend who provided her with inexpensive technology support, that her computer was running slow. Paul, being the softie that he is, returned to her home time and time again, fixed the computer, and warned her about her son's computer habits. This became a vicious cycle until one day Paul couldn't retrieve the data from her crashed hard drive. Her son had downloaded yet another virus. And this virus had hit the mother lode!

Sarah had become lax with her backups and had to spend valuable time rebuilding client files. She finally purchased a new computer that she used exclusively for business. Also, Sarah subscribed to an automatic backup service because she didn't trust herself to keep up with that critical task.

This case happens time and time again. The wisdom to take away from the above case is that the computer that your kids use for games and your spouse uses to store pictures should not be your primary business computer. Having a computer at home is one thing – it's okay for your home computer to be outdated and for you to fail to back it up (maybe). But when you own a business, your technology is an integral part of running your business. It affects you and your employees' productivity. It stores key and potentially confidential information about your customers. Give it the respect that it deserves.

CASE STUDY 7:

Zach's business had recently been awarded a multi-million dollar government contract. He had been using his Cousin Zeke to maintain his computer network since the inception of his business. Unbeknownst to Zach, Cousin Zeke maintained his network for a fraction of the cost of other technicians by piecing together parts from old computers.

When the government contract came through, Zach decided that he could afford to upgrade his network and asked Cousin Zeke to handle the task. Cousin Zeke declined because he allegedly didn't have the expertise to support the new environment. Cousin Zeke felt taken advantage of by Zach and didn't want the burden of getting nickeled and dimed for everything. Zach solicited bids from several vendors and received a rude awakening. Cousin Zeke's $40-per-hour price was one-third the rate he would have to pay the lowest bidder. Furthermore, he had to pay for the new company to correct *the inefficient configuration that Cousin Zeke had pieced together.*

We are all tempted to select the cheapest alternative for everything. However, as Zach learned the hard way, the cheapest solution in the short run is not always the least expensive and most efficient for the long term. The system you have when you're starting might not be the same system you'll need when your business expands. Your best option for a tech savvy guru may not be Cousin Zeke. He may just tell you what you want to hear, not what is best for your business. Invest wisely.

According to my experience, a good technology professional will:

- Tell you the truth about your technology needs and provide you a comprehensive quote to get the job done;

- Seek out the most cost-effective alternatives for you but advise you of the pitfalls of merely selecting the cheapest;

- Insist that you purchase licensed software;

- Not rob you blind but will demand a reasonable fee for the services provided.

If you have just started your company and haven't addressed technology, ask yourself the following:

- Do you have valid licenses for all of the software you are using to run your business, or did you get the hookup from Cousin Zeke?
- Have you been advised that you need new hardware, but you have been making do hoping that it won't crash? Has Cousin Zeke been piecing it together?
- Do your kids use the computer that contains your business information?
- Would it take a lot of time to reconstruct your business information if your computer crashed?
- Are you choosing to pay yourself more than you need to meet your personal obligations, instead of updating your technology?
- Do you run regular backups and have a disaster recovery plan?
- Do you maintain confidential client information?
- Do you know what the reasonable market rate is for a technology consultant in your area?

Don't just run to the local electronics retailer to buy a business computer. Plan and solicit the input of someone who knows technology when you are putting together a network. Do it right the first time, and you won't have to do it over!

TIMTIM.COM

"It's hard for an entrepreneur to be a great manager. Many great entrepreneurs don't know how to balance the books. They need someone to do the financial end of the business. A great entrepreneur and a great manager are usually not the same person. The skills are very different."

--Lillian Vernon -- founder, chairman and chief executive officer of Lillian Vernon Corporation

Hire Professionals

When you launch your business, plan on eventually hiring professionals for certain key tasks such as accounting, technology and legal work. If the only accounting you have ever done is balancing your checkbook, don't try to do your own business books. I know the television commercials and the internet make it seem easy, but when you need to apply for a bank loan or submit financial statements for various certifications, you'll need accurate financials. If your only legal education is watching Law & Order, The Good Wife and Harry's Law, then by all means, don't write your own business contracts. There is a reason why there is an accounting degree, with a grueling certification exam and why being an attorney requires law school and passing a long licensing test.

Time and time again I encounter business owners who have been in business for many years and are muddling through their own books or who think that accounting is just math, so their daughter with a degree in sociology can handle the books. When they attempt to secure a business loan, they have nothing presentable to give the bank because their balance sheet looks like a jigsaw puzzle without all of the pieces intact.

You might think you are unable to afford an accountant when you first start your business. However, it may be more efficient to hire one to ensure that your books are accurate from the beginning than to be forced to hire one at a later date to reconstruct the financial records necessary to generate financial statements your loan officer can decipher. Having to hire a professional at the last minute to redo your concocted financials could take so long that you no longer qualify for that special small-business loan program that the bank was offering for only thirty days. Or you may have to pay more for expedited service. Obviously I am focusing on accounting because I have witnessed books and records that turned my hair grey. (Actually, it was probably time for me to get a grey hair or two, but I like blaming it on something other than age).

CASE STUDY 8:

Harriet was entering into a new phase of business and wanted a CPA who could be a strategic partner and advisor. Her original accountant charged her a nominal monthly fee to generate financial statements, but when she needed business advice, he was nowhere to be found. And quite frankly, Harriet simply filed the monthly financial statements she received because she didn't understand their importance in running her business.

Her friend Gladys also owns a business. Gladys uses a CPA who also acts as her business advisor and assists with many financial decisions. She can call her CPA anytime and expect her call to be returned in a reasonable period of time. Gladys pays her CPA more than twice the fee Harriet pays but feels that her CPA's input into her business decisions is worth every penny. Gladys referred her CPA to Harriet, who quickly arranged a meeting. Harriet was shocked at the quote she received. Even though the CPA had more credentials and included substantially more services in her quote, she just couldn't conceive of paying that much more money. Harriet kept her current arrangement.

Months later when she needed advice on a critical business matter, her accountant pulled the usual disappearing act. When she did reach him days later, she was advised that a discussion of the topic at hand was not part of their arrangement and that she would have to pay substantially more to receive his input.

Harriet was sorry to learn that; overall, it would have been less expensive and more productive to hire the new CPA.

As with technology, the least expensive accountant is not necessarily the cheapest in the long run. You cannot compare apples with oranges. Look at the credentials of the professional you are hiring as well as your business needs.

Consider the following:

- Do you lack the capability within your own organization to perform the function?
- Does the accountant/CPA have expertise in your industry?
- Do they come highly referred by associates that

you trust?

- Do they have additional credentials, along with the CPA (e.g. MBA, JD, MD) that will benefit your organization?

- Will the CPA merely provide you with a report, or do you have access to their wealth of knowledge?

Accurate financial statements are important, and we will address that issue more in an upcoming chapter. However, it is just as important to make sure that an attorney reviews or develops your legal documents. As a business owner, you will sign leases, sign contracts with vendors, develop contracts between you and your customers and establish employment policies and procedures. It may be okay to throw a form or two together using legal tools on the internet, but you have to know when it is time to bring in the big guns and hire an attorney. Small print in a business deal can kill a business, so it is important that someone who understands it reviews it for you to make sure your business doesn't end up dead and buried under dirt and daises.

Documents that can really get you into trouble are employment policies, procedures and handbooks. When starting out with only one employee, it may be acceptable to skip the employee handbook (although I wouldn't recommend it). However, at some point, you will need to address employee-related matters and provide workers with written policies and procedures. Please don't try to write them yourself if you are not an employment attorney or human resources professional. Simply copying some else's handbook is not sufficient. How do you know theirs is correct? There are reasons why large corporations have clearly articulated personnel policies and procedures…it helps keep them out of legal hot water.

CASE STUDY 9:

Jermaine started a business that relied on unskilled labor to service his clients. In the beginning he and Crystal, the employee who had been with him since inception of the business, were able to serve his clientele. However, his business grew to the point that he needed to add ten employees fast. He advertised on Craigslist and soon had a workforce of twelve, including himself.

Several months later, Crystal's husband left her for his secretary, and she became depressed and unable to work for several weeks. Respecting the fact that Crystal had been a loyal employee from day one, Jermaine secured coverage for her shifts and paid her anyway. One of his new employees was Mable, the payroll clerk. When she was entering hours into the payroll system, she inquired about Crystal's hours, and Jermaine, in a rush to get to his next client, told her to pay Crystal for 40 hours. He rushed out of the office before he noticed the surprised expression on Mable's face.

Later that year, Mable decided that she needed some time off, so she called Jermaine and told him that she and her fiancé broke up. She requested a few days off to get her head together. When Jermaine informed her that she would have to take the days off without pay, Mable accused Jermaine of discriminating against her and threatened to file a complaint with the Department of Labor.

Jermaine paid Mable for the three days because it would have been more time consuming and costly to fight her. Mable was able to take advantage of him because he didn't have a documented paid time off policy, and his actions with Crystal led Mable to believe that she could take paid time off for a similar reason.

There are many resources for personnel policies and procedures. Basic policies are available for purchase, and some of the major payroll providers offer a handbook writing service. Find out what policies are critical to your business, and have them written or reviewed by an expert.

Consider the following questions:

- How soon will you need to hire employees?
- Is your business a service business that relies heavily on a workforce?
- Is your company in an industry that experiences high turnover? Does your company experience high turnover?
- Will a large percentage of your workforce be unskilled?
- Do you provide benefits such as sick, vacation and other forms of paid time off?

There comes a time when every business needs to formalize its policies, procedures and contracts. Obviously if you are the only employee, you don't need an employee handbook right away. But keep it in the back of your mind because as soon as you begin to take on staff, a handbook will be essential. If you are working out of your home office, you don't need an attorney to review a lease, but when you decide to move into an office building, you may want to have someone look over the lease.

Hire professionals for key functions, and you will probably save money and avoid costly mistakes in the long run.

"There may be liberty and justice for all, but there are tax breaks only for some."

--Martin A. Sullivan -- Economist

Why Do I Have to Pay Taxes?

It is a fact that if you own a business that is making money, you will be required to pay taxes. In recent months, we have heard about large global companies who use a host of tax loopholes and other mechanisms to avoid paying income taxes. But you can bet your new business, (or should I say your bottom dollar), that you don't have the money or political influence to avoid them like the big boys do. However, even if they do avoid income taxes, these companies all pay payroll taxes. Face it, the old saying is true: nothing is certain but death and taxes.

Most business owners will pay income and/or employment taxes. Since this is such an important area, I will take some time to explain the different types of taxes that most small business owners encounter.

When you have employees, you, as the employer, have certain employment tax responsibilities that you must pay and forms you must file with both the federal and state governments. Employment taxes include Social Security and Medicare taxes, federal and state unemployment taxes, and federal and state income tax withholding. You are responsible for withholding and remitting some of these taxes to the government on behalf of your employees and other taxes such as unemployment taxes are your responsibility. This is another one of those "put you to sleep" topics so go ahead, refresh your coffee and turn to Page 116 of the Appendix if you want the long description. I'll be here when you get back...or you can continue reading the book and get to it a little later.

Failure to pay employment taxes and file the appropriate returns in a timely manner is a quick way to get your business in trouble. If you get behind, it is very difficult to catch up because your liability increases with each payroll. There are also significant penalties and interest charges associated with late filing and payment. As an employer, you are entrusted with the responsibility of remitting the taxes that you withhold from an employee's check to the government in a timely manner. If you don't, you have breached that responsibility and will be penalized. Payroll processing is a cumbersome task. Regardless of the size of your business, it may be more efficient to utilize the services of a payroll-processing company.

I'd like to take the time here to address independent contractors. Many small businesses routinely classify employees as independent contractors because the employer is not required to withhold or pay payroll taxes for independent contractors. This is such a hot topic that the IRS has issued flyers and information defining the difference between an independent contractor and an employee on the IRS website http://www.irs.gov/businesses/small/article/0,,id=187534,00.html

Study these publications and ask your CPA or attorney about your employees' classifications. If you are audited, and it is later determined that you have misclassified employees as independent contractors, it will be a costly mistake. Also, if the contractor is unaware that you are not withholding taxes and you terminate him/her, you may end up with Department of Labor issues.

CASE STUDY 10:

Giovanni owns a business that experiences rapid turnover. She currently has more than fifty workers, and the only ones classified as employees on the payroll are she and Madge, her payroll clerk. Madge insisted that she be placed on the payroll, so she could collect unemployment if the business ever folded. Betsy is the billing contractor, who only works for Giovanni part time, as she has two other large clients as well.

One day Betsy and Giovanni got into a confrontation in front of several other workers. Giovanni decided that Betsy was a liability and fired her on the spot. Betsy argued for severance pay, but Giovanni informed her that she was not an employee and was therefore ineligible for severance (even though there wasn't a severance program in place for employees either). Betsy was furious and filed for unemployment compensation, knowing that Giovanni had not been paying into it for her.

The state where Giovanni's business is located is a pro-employee state. When Betsy's unemployment was denied, red flags went up at the unemployment office, and they audited Giovanni's business. After the audit, they determined that many of her workers should have been classified as employees instead of independent contractors. Giovanni was forced to pay back unemployment taxes on the misclassified workers.

The Department of Labor was Giovanni's next unwanted guest. Betsy had spitefully filed a complaint because she was angry, and it opened Giovanni up for more scrutiny than she could afford.

As illustrated above, sometimes it's better to do the right thing from the beginning. Whether or not a worker should be classified as an employee or an independent contractor is determined by the degree of control you will have over the worker. To help determine the proper classification, the IRS developed a 20 factor test. I won't list everything, because a CPA or attorney can narrow down what's true for your specific case. However, the following are some of the factors that must be considered when classifying a worker:

- *Will the individual receive routine instructions from you or your staff?*

- *Will you determine the sequence of the work they perform, as well as how they perform the work?*

- *Will you be training the individual?*

- *Is the person required to perform the work themselves (i.e. they cannot subcontract the work to someone else)?*

- *Are they required to be on site during prescribed hours? Do you set their schedule?*

- *Will you be paying them by the hour, week or month?*

- *Do you plan to pay their business and/or traveling expenses?*

- *Will you be providing them with the tools to complete*

their assignment (e.g. computer, calculator, paper, pens, etc.)?

If you answered in the affirmative to many of the questions listed above, then your independent contractor may be an employee.

I know I digressed a bit with the discussion above, but the topic of employee classification is something that every business owner should be aware of. In this time of economic hardship, more and more states are looking for new ways to generate revenue. One way is through additional payroll taxes, fines and penalties associated with employee misclassification.

Let's get back to our exciting discussion of taxes. The next tax I will address is the business income tax. Some small business owners think that they should not have to pay any income taxes associated with their businesses, even when they are earning large sums of money. It is important to remember that after you incorporate, the business is a separate entity from you, and that entity is required to file federal and state income tax returns. The type of business income tax return that you file will depend on the business structure you selected.

Unless you are a C-Corporation, your business tax return will affect your personal tax return. You will receive a K-1 from your business, reflecting your share of the company's earnings, losses and distributions (assuming that you get your corporate taxes prepared). It is very important to tell your tax preparer if you have joined a Partnership or LLC or started a business during the year. When you own a business you can no longer just run to your local tax guy and get your personal taxes done the day you receive your W-2. You have to wait until the K-1 from your business is complete. In order for your K-1 to be complete, your business tax return must be complete. And your business tax return is prepared from your business financial statements; which means that you need to actually have financial statements.

Now I know many of you have a wonderful tax guy (don't mean to be sexist but guy fits better into the paragraph!). You just throw all of your business receipts in a shoebox, take them to your tax guy and—presto! — You have a tax return. Who needs an accountant throughout the year? Eventually, you will. Your business will grow to a point that your tax guy won't have the time or desire to sift through your box of receipts during tax season. Furthermore, financial statements serve a useful purpose to the business beyond just completing a tax return. They should be used to help you make business decisions! We'll address the usefulness of financial statements in more detail in an upcoming chapter.

CASE STUDY 11:

Levi is a mortgage broker. Several years ago, he incorporated his business because he wanted to protect his personal assets. He was advised to file the Subchapter S election form, and he did so without really knowing what that meant. He notified all the companies he did business with of his new tax identification number and thought nothing more about the matter. He didn't know he needed to tell Cousin Bob, his tax preparer, about this new development, and Cousin Bob didn't ask any questions. After all, he was an insurance salesman and only did taxes for his relatives to earn extra money during the tax season. He charged them a lot less than H&R Block, so he didn't think he needed to go the extra mile.

Every year, shortly after Levi received his W-2, Cousin Bob prepared and e-filed his personal tax return. Levi always got a hefty refund and was thrilled with Cousin Bob. Four years after incorporating, Levi received notification from the IRS that he had failed to file multiple years of corporate tax returns. He went to Cousin Bob, who promptly informed him that he didn't know anything about corporate taxes and didn't even know that Levi had a corporation.

Levi was terrified of the IRS letters he was receiving and went to a local CPA who asked him for his financial statements for the business. Levi had never prepared financial statements; therefore the CPA had to prepare four years of financial statements from Levi's bank statements and a grocery bag of receipts that he was thankful he had retained. The end result was that the S-Corporation had experienced net income since incorporation. Levi had made many cash withdrawals that he couldn't account for and had never paid himself a salary or any estimated taxes. The income from the S-Corporation needed to be reported on his personal tax return, so the CPA prepared four years of amended personal tax returns to account for the business income.

Levi now had a large tax bill and no longer spoke to Cousin Bob.

The lesson from Levi's situation is that tax preparers are only as good as the information you give them. If you started a business or joined a Partnership, LLC, LLP, or any other business (with the exception of a C-Corporation) you will receive a K-1. You have to give this K-1 to your tax preparer. Business tax returns are not due until the middle of March, so you can't have your personal tax returns prepared until your K-1 has been generated. Rushing to the tax guy in January is no longer an option!

I'd like to point out here that your income tax refund should not be considered a bonus or your method of saving money. Your goal should be to break even at the end of the year. If you get a big refund, perhaps you have given the government an interest-free loan. Work with your accountant to do some tax planning, so you are using your own money throughout the year instead of letting the IRS, which really doesn't need that "unintended loan", have a party at your expense.

I would be remiss if I didn't address correspondence from taxing authorities. Throughout the years, I am always amazed at the number of business owners who bring unopened correspondence from the IRS to my office. Often the letters are several months old and a second or third request is in the stack. By the time I get them, the problem is worse than it would have been had they taken the time to open the letters and respond accordingly.

If you own a business, you will receive correspondence from the Internal Revenue Service, as well as from your state department of revenue and unemployment agency. Sometimes, the letters are merely forms or general correspondence. However, some of the letters you will receive will require action on your part. These letters more often than not have a deadline by which you must make a payment, sign a document or handle a myriad possible tax-related situations. Don't get nervous and simply ignore IRS correspondence. The situation gets worse the longer you ignore it. Open it immediately!

Remember the following:

- Store all of your tax documents in the same place each year, so they will be readily available for your tax preparer. You shouldn't have to wait until the last minute to file your taxes because you misplaced everything.
- Understand that at some point it will be advantageous to have routine financial statements prepared for your business to facilitate timely tax planning and decision-making.
- If you elect to defer having routine financial statements prepared throughout the year, at least summarize and organize your receipts for your tax preparer.
- Consider using a payroll-processing company to process your payroll, remit your employment taxes and prepare your quarterly and annual returns.
- Take care to appropriately classify your workers (independent contractors versus employees).
- DON'T IGNORE IRS LETTERS!

"In a family business, it's the third generation that presents the big problems. The first generation founds the company and has the drive and the dedication to move it forward. The second generation rides that wave. The third generation wants to do their own thing. They've seen Broadway; they've had all the advantages."
    --Gale Petronis,
    President of Amazon Hose & Rubber Co of Miami

    "It is easier to build strong children than to repair broken men." ---Frederick Douglass

The "Not My Child" Syndrome

On occasion, local news stations feature stories in which a teen accused of a heinous crime is being carted off by the police in handcuffs. In the background a hysterical mother is insisting, "Not my child. He's a good boy." Meanwhile, the whole neighborhood knows that the boy was setting fire to the neighborhood wildlife or selling drugs on the street corner, but the mother is in denial or doesn't want to believe that her child could commit such a serious crime. I refer to this as the "Not My Child" Syndrome.

Now, I know that everyone has wonderful children whom they love (well, at least most of the time). You want your children to have a better life than you had, so you are building a business as your legacy. Your child has always expressed an interest in teaching, but you have purchased a fast food franchise. Although your child is a bit difficult at times and can't keep friends, you hope that will change when they are added to your management team. So you insert your child into the business in a critical position.

When something serious falls through the cracks, and other employees gently try to inform you that it was your child who failed to perform, you get a shocked expression on your face and ignore the error. You make everyone else pay for the mistake because you refuse to accept the fact that your child was negligent with his or her responsibilities. Eventually, even your child's supervisor does not critique his/her performance; your child's errors are covered up, and others make up for the deficiencies. Your company is suffering from the "Not My Child" Syndrome.

Now, this syndrome is not limited to just the children of the owners. It includes close relatives, such as sisters, brothers, husbands, ex-husbands, and anyone else with whom you have an emotional attachment. In 'The Naked Truth of Owning a Business' (final shameless plug!), I touched on this topic, but since this book is for those of you who have decided to move into the implementation phase of your business, I am addressing it in greater detail.

I think it's wonderful when children, sisters, aunts, uncles and cousins twice removed are engaged in a family business. If you can't trust your family, who can you trust, right? It's a wonderful idea, and when it works, it can be good for the business. In most cases, your family will be loyal and dedicated, but hiring them will only work when they are qualified to do the job. However, when you have the "Not My Child" Syndrome, you think your loved ones can do anything and fail to accept the reality of their shortcomings. When your loved one is clearly a problem, and you ignore that problem, your business will suffer.

CASE STUDY 12:

Jake and his daughter, Cassidy, are joint partners in a service business. Jake owns 51 percent of the business and Cassidy owns 49 percent. Jake insisted on majority ownership because he felt that, as a seasoned business professional, he would need to override Cassidy's business decisions from time to time. They worked well together for several years.

In their third year of business, Cassidy decided that she didn't really like the business they were in and wanted to do something different with her life. However, she didn't really want to tell her father. So instead, she came into the office less and less. She also enrolled in several educational programs to try to find out what she really wanted to do. Because she hated her job so much, she wasn't getting her work done during the brief time she did appear at the office. She was responsible for the financial functions of the company, and her lack of attention was beginning to take a toll on the business. The stress from working a job that she despised, being consistently behind schedule with her responsibilities, and dealing with a crumbling marriage, contributed to her having a nervous breakdown and being hospitalized for an extended period.

Jake was aware of the fact that Cassidy was a burden to the business but figured that when she got better she would be more dedicated to her job. During her absence, he hired an accountant to keep the books up to date and provide much needed advice and guidance. The atmosphere was less chaotic and everything was running more smoothly than ever.

However, Cassidy began to feel left out and wanted to come back to work. Because she was a partner in the business, Jake welcomed her back. The loyal accountant who had maintained their finances for more than a year while his daughter recovered was released from his position.

Cassidy came back to work, but a short time later started hating the job again and began to shorten her work hours. The cycle repeated itself. The company is still in business, but the father is struggling to hold it together without the support of his daughter. Even though he knows better, he won't remove his daughter from her position.

The father in the above case is suffering from the "Not My Child" Syndrome. Even though his daughter demonstrated through her behavior that she is not an asset to the business, he refuses to accept that fact. If you are starting out your business and there is a possibility that you could suffer from the "Not My Child" Syndrome, ask yourself the following questions before you put a loved one on the payroll:

- Do they possess the skills and education necessary to function effectively in the job that I am putting them in?
- Would I hire them in the position if they were not related to me?
- Are they truly interested in working in my business or have they been unable to hold down a job working for others?
- Am I truly able to hear constructive criticism

about my family without punishing the person who delivered the criticism?

- Am I planning on paying them significantly more than the market dictates?
- Will hiring them and paying them more than market cause me to be unable to fill other critical positions within the company?
- Will I be able to keep personal family business out of the workplace if I hire family members?

It's important to understand your motivation for hiring a loved one. If you are aware of their strengths and deficiencies, you will be better able to position them in your organization. Don't hide your head in the sand where your loved one is concerned. If they lack the skills and capabilities that your company needs, then don't put them in a critical management position. If they have poor leadership and customer service skills and are difficult to get along with, make them an individual contributor. Don't have skilled workers report to them. It is an insult when a more experienced, skilled professional is forced to report to your child who has no expertise in the area. The skilled professional will probably be looking for a new job the entire time they are working for you. The saying goes, "business before pleasure," but in this case it's business before family.

"If we are together nothing is impossible. If we are divided all will fail." --Winston Churchill

Don't Do a Deal with the Devil

When your business becomes a success, you may need the support of an investor to take you to the next level. Investors can be very helpful to your business and may be the only alternative for significant expansion. However, don't do a deal with the Devil. I know this statement sounds extreme, but when you are selling a portion of your business, it is just as important that you know who you are dealing with as it is for the investor to do his or her due diligence. Just because your potential investor has money and is willing to invest in your company does not mean that they share your value system or your goals for the business. Make no mistake, investors are in it for the money; they don't care about your overwhelming need to change the world or your ability to leap tall buildings in a single bound. They don't care if you're a bird, a plane or…you get the point. They expect to be repaid and to make a generous return on their investment for the risk that they are taking.

An investor is not your new best friend. Let me stress this one more time…an investor IS NOT your new best friend. Of course investors will be helpful to you and may provide leadership and support. They may even be on your board of directors or insist that you hire a particular executive who has expertise that you lack. However, while they might be seen as the knights in shining armor who enable you to grow your business, they can also be like the Devil if you mess up the money end of things.

When you take their money, there will be restrictions associated with that money so make sure that you have done your homework before you sign on the dotted line.

This is a case where you need a good, experienced attorney. Make sure that the restrictive covenants and repayments to the investor will not be so excessive that the infusion of capital into your business ultimately hinders your business more than it helps. Getting $5 million to grow your business can be a welcomed windfall, but if the repayment terms prevent you from effectively servicing your customers; it is not a good business deal.

CASE STUDY 13:

Crystal, Cathy and Candy started a technology company ten years ago, with each owning one-third of the business. They prepared their own operating agreement and never updated it or had it reviewed by an attorney. After years and years of hard work, the company boasted more than $75 million per year in sales, and the owners were enjoying the fruits of their labor. They purchased a corporate yacht, and Crystal and Candy frequently took cruises together along the Caribbean and the Hawaiian islands. Cathy developed a passion for French cuisine and relocated to France. They paid themselves lavish bonuses and enjoyed the good life. They had confidence in their leadership team and held weekly conference *calls with them, where they were assured that all was well with the business. However, all was not well.*

While Candy and Crystal cruised on the company yacht, Cathy began to feel rejected and lost interest in the business. Without discussing it with Candy and Crystal, Cathy sold her third of the business to an investor. At the time, the two million dollars she received for her shares seemed reasonable. She didn't think she was doing anything wrong because the investor agreed to infuse millions of dollars into the company for cash-flow purposes. It all sounded good to Cathy, so she signed on the dotted line without an attorney's review.

Crystal and Candy did not know they had a new business partner until it was too late. They decided to make the best of the shocking situation and met with the new partner. To their horror, they learned that the agreement Cathy signed required that they maintain certain financial ratios that hampered their ability to make the sizeable technology purchases necessary to support their expansion. Their inability to invest in their infrastructure negatively impacted customer service. They ran a web-hosting company that was unable to purchase sufficient storage to support both their existing and new clients.

As a result of the storage issues, employees began to wonder what was going on with the company. The company began to experience excessive turnover in their customer service division because inadequate storage created numerous problems in customer networks. The customer service representatives were forced to constantly explain why the system was slow and why backups continued to fail.

Over time, the remaining two partners were forced to sell some of their shares in the company to the investor just so they would be able to purchase additional storage. The end result was that the investor owned a controlling interest, and Crystal and Candy were no longer the primary decision makers for the company they started.

The above case has many lessons. Some I have already addressed in other chapters, but they bear repeating. Others will open your eyes to the need to hire qualified professionals to assist you with your business.

Lesson 1:

You must have an operating/shareholder/partnership agreement with an exit clause that spells out the conditions for getting out of the agreement. Cathy should not have been able to sell her share of the business without the consent or, at a minimum, the knowledge of her other partners. The operating/shareholder/ partnership agreement should have given the partners the right of first refusal or, at a minimum, the ability to approve the buyer.

Lesson 2:

Always hire an attorney to translate the fine print in important documents. An agreement that outlines something as important as the sale of shares of stock in your business should be reviewed closely by an attorney knowledgeable about corporate matters.

Lesson 3:

Cathy may have sold her shares for less than their value. She should have hired a CPA to complete a business valuation.

Lesson 4:

Candy and Crystal lost touch with Cathy. They did not maintain a relationship that was close enough to affect Cathy's decision to sell. If they had maintained closer contact, she probably would have shared her intentions to sell with them before she took the plunge.

Lesson 5:

Although Candy and Crystal made excellent salaries, they did not amass personal wealth. If they had, they would have at least had the option to loan the company the funds to purchase the additional storage needed to effectively service their clients and maintain their hold on the company.

"The biggest mistake was that I did not hire all the right people…"
--Lilian Vernon,
founder, chairman and CEO of Lillian Vernon Corporation

Avoid Creating Bait and Switch Jobs

Now that you are launching your business, you will more than likely need to hire employees and/or contractors. When you do, resist the temptation to create "bait and switch" jobs. I define "bait and switch" jobs as those where you describe one job and one level of expertise during the interview, but when the candidate decides to take the job, it morphs into another job, one that generally would have required a higher skill level and paid a higher wage.

As a startup business, you will (or should) be frugal with your financial resources. As a result, you may want the bookkeeper to act as your chief financial officer (CFO) or your receptionist to also be your customer service representative, but this is not always practical. First, if you want a CFO, hire a CFO. The CFO can also be the bookkeeper, but the reverse is not necessarily true. A candidate with solid customer service skills may be able to double as the receptionist, but a receptionist may not possess the skills to handle customer service issues.

When you develop a job description, make sure it describes the position that you actually want to fill, not the dream job that you think the candidate wants. When you perform interviews, be truthful. Advise the accountant or CFO candidate that their job will also include bookkeeping responsibilities. Don't get them in the door by advertising "the perfect" CFO position when all you really have is a bookkeeping position that may eventually evolve into a CFO. Keep in mind that employees are not necessarily interchangeable, especially without additional training and education, and small businesses don't always have the budget to provide training. Just because Betsy, your receptionist, quit, does not mean that Jill, the bookkeeper, can be moved into her position because you believe Jill has some down time during the day. Bookkeeping requires concentration, and asking that your bookkeeper answer the phone could set him or her up to fail.

CASE STUDY 14:

Carmen was hired to head up the nursing division of a healthcare company. She was highly qualified and excited about the new opportunities and challenges she would have on the new job. She had left a good position at an insurance company but felt she had made the best decision based on what the owner of the company had shared with her during the interview. Although the written job description was vague and somewhat mundane, the owner had assured her over dinner that she would be an integral part of the team that would manage a new contract that was supposed to materialize in the near future. With that contract, Carmen was assured a pay increase and additional responsibilities that would significantly enhance her resume.

However, after working her new job for seven months, Carmen realized that there was no contract on the horizon. Her new job was more mundane than her previous position, which meant she wasn't using many of her skills and capabilities. She regretted mak-

ing the job change and began looking for a new, more challenging opportunity.

After less than a year on the job, the owner was both per-plexed and angry when Carmen resigned and returned to a job at an insurance company.

In the case above, Carmen experienced the "bait and switch" job. She was presented with a job that she was excited about, only to find out that what was described to her at the interview was merely a figment of the owner's imagination.

The mistake that the owner made in the case above is obvious. Instead of interviewing the candidate based on the actual job description, the owner presented a job based on future dreams and plans. It's wonderful to be a visionary, but when you are hiring for a particular job; your discussions should focus on the current job description. It is okay to share your goals for the position, but resist the temptation to elaborate to make the job seem something that it isn't. If you are looking at a candidate for a future position, make sure that you tell them that the job today is what the job description outlines, but that within a specified period of time you may be able to redesign their position. Be honest and let them know that there is no guarantee that this will happen.

In addition to baiting and switching during the hiring process, some business owners make poor personnel changes that disrupt a business that was running smoothly.

CASE STUDY 15:

Marilyn worked for her parents in the family-owned business. She had a college degree in business administration and was a reasonably hardworking employee when properly supervised, but she tended to spend a lot of time on Facebook when she was left to her own devices. She was still in her twenties and single, so she liked to go out during the week with her friends. For several years, she had handled accounts payable and payroll for the business. She enjoyed her position and knew that she couldn't really handle any more responsibility.

Marilyn reported to a highly experienced CFO, who closely supervised and trained her on general accounting. To make her job easier, the CFO standardized all monthly financial transactions, requiring that Marilyn merely change the amounts each month. Although Marilyn entered the transactions into the accounting system, she really didn't understand them. When circumstances required that the standardized transactions be modified, the CFO made the adjustments, and Marilyn would keypunch them.

Marilyn's parents thought that her accounting role was greater than what it actually was. When they asked Marilyn if she could handle the CFO position, Marilyn assured them that she could. After all, it would mean a substantial pay increase, and she needed the money to pay off her credit card balances that had increased dramatically due to her internet shopping. Her parents let the CFO go and promoted Marilyn to his position.

All appeared to be going well until they failed to meet payroll and needed financial statements for a business line of credit. When the line of credit was denied based in part on the incoherent balance sheet that Marilyn prepared, her parents were furious. During their heated exchange, Marilyn repeatedly told them that she was not an accountant and shouldn't have been expected to do financial statements.

Marilyn's parents were forced to hire an accountant who they made report to Marilyn, setting her up for another disaster when the new accountant realized that Marilyn understood accounting about as well as a parrot actually understands what it is saying.

In the case above, Marilyn's parents made several mistakes:

They didn't recognize the value of their CFO until it was too late. They were unaware that their CFO's job responsibilities encompassed more than accounting. Cash flow management was also his responsibility, and he had managed it well.

They took for granted that money would be in the bank for payroll and hadn't realized that the CFO's astute cash management was the reason it always had been. They were also unaware that he had been maintaining a close relationship with their banker and was well aware of the requirements for a business line of credit.

They overvalued the contribution of their daughter. They took her word regarding her accounting skills. They knew she didn't have a degree in accounting and should have understood that she would not be able to perform. (She either didn't know what she didn't know or was so blinded by money that she blatantly fibbed to her parents about her abilities.)

Know the value of your employees before you decide to make any dramatic changes. Also, just because your child thinks he or she can handle a particular job doesn't mean that they can, particularly if they do not have the education to perform the function. Test them out first; solicit the opinion of their supervisor. Marilyn's parents should have sent her back to school for additional coursework, which may have better prepared her for the CFO position.

CASE STUDY 16:

Joshua was the manager of more than fifty employees in a small, but growing, business. On the surface, Joshua's job appeared routine. On paper it was very specific, and the responsibilities were clear. However, the job was more challenging than the job description implied because it required excellent customer service, negotiation and leadership skills. The customer base was very particular and complained incessantly about their services, even when there wasn't really a problem. Joshua was often required to intercede between customers and employees. The business was in an industry where there was a severe shortage in skilled labor, so the needs of the employees had to be considered when resolving customer service issues. Joshua was able to satisfy all parties and was so good at his job that he made it look easy.

Bessie, the owner of the business, had been pondering ways to make more money for several months. The business was running smoothly, so she had selected a vacation home in the Caribbean to purchase. However, she needed more income to qualify for another mortgage. She reviewed the salaries of all of her employees and quickly decided that Joshua was overpaid. She surmised that she could replace him with a lower cost manager. She hatched a plan to make his position part-time to force him to resign. She knew that he needed a full-time job to take care of his family. However, much to her chagrin, Joshua accepted the part-time position. What she didn't know at the time was that Joshua had only accepted the part-time position until he found another job. So several weeks later, Joshua submitted his resignation after accepting a similar position with a competitor.

Bessie was overjoyed that her plan had worked. She interviewed new managers, making the job sound easier than it actually was because she was unaware of all the customer service requirements of the job. A less experienced candidate eagerly accepted the position at a salary thirty thousand dollars less than what Joshua had been paid. Bessie increased her salary by thirty thousand dollars and purchased the vacation home.

Six months later, Bessie was shocked when many of her best clients informed her that they would no longer need her services. To make matters worse, a dozen employees were submitting their resignations. When she investigated, she learned that her new manager lacked the necessary people skills and couldn't negotiate getting a Big Mac at McDonald's! The employees hated their new manager, and her customers were outraged that Joshua had been replaced.

Bessie's new vacation home sits empty because now she has to work more to cover the inadequacies of her new manager.

The lessons from the case above are clear. Bessie made a number of mistakes.

She allowed greed to lead to a poorly thought out business decision.

She lost touch with what it took to accomplish the tasks of a key position in her company. She assumed that everything was the same as it was when she started the business and that the job was easier than it was.

She failed to realize that when she eliminated Joshua, the customers and employees with whom he had a good working relationship would react.

She was more concerned with her own personal luxury than the well-being of her employees.

I know you are probably surprised by number four. You are thinking, "I AM starting the business for personal wealth!" Yes, we all start businesses, in part, because we want to improve our lives. However, as a small business owner, it is my opinion that your employees are usually as important, and in some cases more important than you are. As your business grows, you won't be able to run it without good help. You should not risk losing a valuable employee just so you can pay yourself more if you are already making ends meet. At that point you're likely to "meet the end." A vacation home is nice, but it could have waited. It is better to have a comfortable life with time to enjoy the fruits of your labor than make a boatload of cash and never have any time to enjoy it.

"The entrepreneur builds an enterprise;
the technician builds a job."

> --Michael Gerber,
> author and movtivational speaker

Don't Create a Job if You Want a Business

I firmly believe that a business is not created when an independent contractor simply decides to incorporate–that's the definition of a job. I consider a business to be an enterprise that can operate for a period of time in the absence of the owner. It will maintain employees, an office, solicit clients, etc. It is very easy to start a business, but with the wrong moves, it can end up being a "job" for you, and not necessarily one that you enjoy.

When I first started my CPA firm, it quickly transformed into a job. Although I was incorporated, had an office, purchased insurance, and ran a payroll for myself, I was working seven days a week for thirty hours each day (Okay, maybe only fourteen hours or so, but it sure felt like thirty!). I was absolutely miserable. I enjoyed what I was doing but was required to do too much of it. I soon realized that if I wanted my business to grow and still have a life, I needed to add staff and delegate some of my workload or I might as well go get a better paying job in Corporate America.

Realizing that I wanted a business and not a job disguised as a business, I cut my pay and hired my first employee—someone with no bookkeeping experience. This is a little off the subject, but I hired a loyal, ethical, hardworking individual who had no bookkeeping experience and trained her myself. I feel that loyalty and dedication can often be more important than someone who is experienced and who will only work for you long enough to get some recent experience on their resume. When looking for workers, I strongly believe that the character of the prospective employee can be more important than experience. Obviously I don't mean that you should hire a receptionist if you need a technology professional, but there are some jobs that a person can perform with minimal training. The key is to not try to train them beyond their capability. Listen to them when they tell you what they can and want to do. Forcing them to do a job that they neither want nor have the skills to perform will only hurt your business (review the chapter on bait and switch jobs). I did not try to turn my bookkeeper into an accountant. I hired an accountant for that job.

Anyway, after my new bookkeeper was fully trained, it was amazing how much of my time was freed up to grow the business!

CASE STUDY 17:

Della is a licensed CPA. She left her job in Corporate America fifteen years ago and is contracting her services out as a CPA. She is not incorporated and records all of her income and expenses on her personal tax return. She has no professional liability insurance and operates out of her home office. She receives a combination of W-2s and 1099s from her customers for the services she provides.

Della is often behind in her workload because it is difficult for her to personally service all of her clients. Furthermore, she is unable to accept additional clients because there is only so much work one person can do. In spite of the fact that she is always late with her client's financial information, she refuses to hire anyone to assist her. She prefers to keep all the fees herself.

One year, Della became very ill and was unable to work for several months. She was forced to temporarily send her clients to other practitioners. Unfortunately, when she was able to resume working, she found out that her clients preferred their new accountants, which meant she was forced to start all over again.

Although Della insists that she is running a business, in my opinion she is both an independent contractor and a part-time employee. And her "business" will die with her. If she had been running a business, she probably would have had other accountants and/or bookkeepers who could have helped her keep her clients while she was on the mend.

If you are planning to start a business make sure that you plan appropriately.

- Formalize the business (e.g. incorporate).
- Purchase the appropriate business insurance for your industry.
- Acquire all business licenses and certifications necessary for your business.
- Hire a staff when you realize that your workload is so heavy that you can no longer network or work on growing your business. This may require that you temporarily cut your salary, but it will be worth it in the long run.

TIMTIM.COM

"Face reality as it is, not as it was or as you wish it to be."
--Jack Welch, past chairman and CEO of General Electric

Listen to the Right People

When you start a business, everyone has something to say about it. You will receive unsolicited advice from people you didn't know were aware you had a business. Of course there are the naysayers who tell you that you should just go get a real job. Then there is the crowd of friends and relatives who want you to give them a job (In 'The Naked Truth of Owning a Business', there's a chapter on hiring hacks. Oh, shoot, another shameless plug slipped up on me!) Those groups are fairly harmless. You can always ignore your parents, who are old school and think it's in your best interest to work for a large corporation so you can have a pension. They don't realize that corporate pension plans are now as extinct as dinosaurs. And with the way our elected officials are tinkering with social security…it's fair to say that it might not stick around to socially secure anything. It's also fairly easy to laugh off your best friend's husband's brother, who hasn't been able to find a decent job since he quit his last job ten years ago in a fit of drunken rage. It's the people who think they know everything about running a business that can be the most harmful.

As a business owner, you'll need to sift through the information and separate the myths and misinformation from the valuable nuggets of advice. You have to listen to the right people.

For example, if your tax preparer advises you one way and your friend's tax preparer tells him or her something entirely different, it's important that you question your tax preparer before acting on your friend's hearsay nugget. Know that your tax preparer is not necessarily wrong. There are a host of issues that must be considered when rendering tax advice, so something that works for your friend may not be the right course of action for you.

CASE STUDY 18:

Veronica owned a profitable business, which allowed her to enjoy many luxuries. One evening, Veronica attended a networking event of business owners with her friend Claire. Claire was holding a rather serious-looking conversation with her friend Zoey, so Veronica decided to move closer to "ear hustle" (the modern day version of eavesdropping). Veronica caught the tail end of the conversation and only heard the part where Claire told Zoey that her tax advisor had told her to take all the money out of her business before the end of the year. Unfortunately for Veronica, she did not hear the entire conversation.

The following Monday, Veronica directed her bookkeeper to write her a check for most of the balance in the corporate checking account. When she deposited the large six figure check, she eagerly thought about the new top-of-the-line BMW convertible that she had been looking at for several months and the new designer wardrobe she needed since she had lost twenty pounds.

Over the next few months, Veronica shopped and shopped

and shopped. It didn't dawn on her to save any of the money. Then one day, Veronica couldn't meet her payroll. When she yelled at her bookkeeper, the bookkeeper reminded her that she was the one who took the entire cash cushion out of the company. Veronica called Claire, confessed about the eavesdropping episode and asked where she had gone wrong. Claire advised her that, while her tax advisor had told her to remove money from the corporation, he made that recommendation with the understanding that she was a very conscientious saver and would be able to infuse capital into her business if it experienced cash-flow difficulties.

As unbelievable as the above case sounds, it's true. The same advice does not apply to everyone. A trusted advisor may tell a business owner who is a disciplined saver to take more from their company. That person will save the money so that it is available if the company experiences cash-flow deficiencies. An advisor may not recommend that an owner who spends recklessly withdraw a large sum of money from the business because that owner may spend it all, leaving no working capital for the business. You have to listen to your own advisors. Hopefully they know your habits and can guide you according to what is best for you and your company.

CASE STUDY 19:

In ten years, Tammy's service business had grown to the point where she was raking in five million dollars per year. She hired a leadership team with whom she brainstormed her strategic ideas. Her team was comprised of experienced professionals who had expertise in many areas, including business development. Her business had grown slowly and steadily, but Tammy wanted it to grow much faster. She remembered that she had worked for a company in the same industry fifteen years earlier, and that company made boatloads of cash providing a service that she didn't offer. The company in question made money hand over fist, and all the executives were lavishly compensated.

She convened her leadership team and requested that they develop a business plan to provide the service that her previous employer had provided. The members of the leadership team spent weeks researching the service and developed a comprehensive business plan. The result of their research was that this particular service was no longer realistic in the current competitive environment and that most potential customers no longer outsourced this to outside firms.

Tammy refused to accept their conclusions and forged ahead with the new line of business. She hired an experienced marketer who developed glossy brochures and marketing materials to introduce the new product. Her new marketing representative mentioned to Tammy that he didn't think that the service she was pursuing was a realistic offering. But he thought that she had done her research, so he came on board anyway.

Fifty thousand dollars later, Tammy fired the marketing representative and scrapped her plans for the new line of business. After several sales meetings with prospective customers, it had become apparent that no one was buying what she was selling.

Keep in mind the following:

- If you hire professionals to support your business, listen to their advice. They are not always going to tell you what you want to hear. Hopefully you have hired the right consultants who will tell you what you need to hear.
- Resist the temptation to always be right. If something you think is a good idea turns out to be a poor one, accept that fact. Don't run full steam ahead anyway.
- Remain current with the trends and competitive environment in your industry. Resist the temptation to try to relive days gone by. The marketplace evolves swiftly so don't try to rely on facts from decades ago to support a current business idea or decision.

timtim.com

"Better three hours too soon, than one minute too late."

--William Shakespeare

Don't Waste Time

Time means money, so don't waste your time or anybody else's. If you want to be perceived as a serious business owner, you should make every effort to be on time for your business appointments. When you make an appointment with another professional, they have scheduled their day around your appointment. Perhaps they had to turn down another meeting to accommodate yours or maybe they were planning on taking a much needed day off...but you ruined their day by blowing off a meeting.

Keep in mind that it is very disrespectful to schedule a meeting with someone and fail to show up without having the decency to at least call and cancel. If the person you are scheduled to meet is not important enough for you to be on time for or even show up, you probably should not be meeting with them in the first place.

My business is a service business which requires that I frequently meet with potential clients. I always prepare for each meeting by researching the client's business and preparing contracts and sample documents. I am prepared for them to sign on the dotted line if they like what they hear. If they fail to show up for the meeting, I have wasted several hours of time that could have been devoted to another client.

In my experience, a business owner who fails to be on time or show up for an appointment will probably be a problematic client. If you can't even be on time or show up to the initial appointment, you will probably be late with everything else.

In my line of work, when my clients are late, it can mean…

- Running to my office at the last minute to get your tax return done because you couldn't pull your documents together;
- Forgetting to file your annual report with the Secretary of State and having your corporation involuntarily dissolved;
- Failing to get your accounting information to me in a timely manner so your financial statements can be completed;
- Ignoring tax communication for several months and then expecting me to work miracles overnight;
- And last but not least, failing to pay your bills (me!) on time.

If you take your business seriously, you will be punctual. Barring a death in the family or your hospitalization, there are few reasons to miss or be late to an appointment. And there is absolutely no excuse for failing to call to inform the other party that you are going to be late or to reschedule.

CASE STUDY 20:

Ron was delinquent with both his payroll and income taxes. He had been using a payroll processor to submit his payroll tax returns and pay the taxes due, but had been kicked off the service because of numerous occurrences of insufficient funds. His account had insufficient funds because he kept forgetting to transfer money to the payroll account in a timely manner. Ron didn't know that his payroll taxes weren't being handled because he never bothered to open the envelopes delivered to him by the payroll company. Furthermore, he never got around to sending the information to his CPA so the CPA could prepare his income taxes. As a result, Ron failed to file corporate income taxes for four years. After numerous calls, emails and missed appointments, his CPA gave up and stopped calling.

Soon Ron noticed that the direct deposits being made by his largest client were consistently less than what he had billed. When Ron called the customer, he was informed that his payments were being garnished due to a five-figure tax levy. The customer further informed him that they had forwarded a copy of the IRS paperwork to him and were shocked that he had not contacted them or attempted to resolve the matter. (Ron failed to pay attention to that paperwork as well.)

After skipping numerous appointments and ignoring phone calls from his CPA, Ron was now frantically trying to get an appointment. However, it was the middle of tax season, and the CPA did not have time to drop all of his other, more punctual and timely clients to resolve Ron's "emergency" issues. The CPA referred Ron to a larger CPA firm that had the manpower to handle Ron's urgent problems. Unfortunately for Ron, the fee was much higher than what his CPA normally charged.

In the case above, Ron learned that time is money. Although he blew off the CPA who had been helping him since he started his business and who was charging him a below market price, he ended up losing that relationship.

As you move to launch your business ask yourself the following:

- Why am I always late for appointments? Is it because I am disorganized?
- Am I capable of changing my incessant tardiness?
- How do I feel when someone is late to one of my appointments?
- What do I need to change about myself to become more punctual before I launch my business?

timtim.com

"Happiness is a positive cash flow."

--Fred Adler, Medical doctor, psychotherapist

Cash is King

Financial management is critical to all businesses, but it is particularly important to small businesses where cash flow can disappear faster than a friend who owes you money. Many businesses that fail in the first year do so because of insufficient cash flow. Your business may be profitable on paper because you have a high volume of receivables, but you can't spend the money until the cash is in the bank. In a small business, cash is king!

When you own a business, financial discipline is critical in both your business and your personal life. Now some of you are probably thinking, "What does she mean by financial discipline?" I'm so glad you asked. You have financial discipline when you have personal savings and make savings a priority or, at a bare minimum, have a personal savings plan. You exercise spending restraint and as a result have a good personal credit score. You don't have an excessive number of credit cards on which you are only paying the minimums. You don't impulse shop and therefore don't continuously buy things that you don't need and can't pay for.

For your business, financial discipline means that you separate your personal expenses from your business expenses. Additionally, it means that you file and pay all of your taxes in a timely manner, pay your employees and vendors on time, and don't spend money that you don't have. You resist the temptation to spend more than you need to on office furnishings and equipment. It's nice to have a beautiful office, but a used leather chair that you purchase from a company that is going out of business will be just as comfortable as that new, high-end chair that costs twice as much.

Even the most disciplined small-business owner will be concerned about cash flow at some point and may have to rely on their personal savings to make ends meet.

CASE STUDY 21:

Henry cashed in all of his retirement savings to start an eye clinic. He had not prepared a budget or consulted with an accountant prior to opening the store because he felt certain that his fifteen years working for a major eyeglass chain had adequately prepared him for running his own business.

Henry rented a corner storefront in an up-and-coming community, purchased top of the line furniture, fixtures and equipment, and hired an interior decorator to ensure that his office was pleasing to the eye (no pun intended). His inventory of eyeglass frames was displayed in luxurious solid oak cabinetry.

After being open for almost a year, Henry began experiencing severe cash-flow problems and consulted with a CPA. After reviewing his records, the CPA concluded that Henry's business was bankrupt. His debts far exceeded his assets and he had obligated his business to monthly expenditures well in excess of what he could expect to take in. He had not done any market research and was unaware at the time he signed his office lease that a well-known competitor with better pricing for the same merchandise was just a few blocks away.

Henry didn't have any additional funds to invest in the business because he had exhausted his savings on leasehold improvements, furnishings and equipment. At the urging of his angry wife, he closed his business within two years and is again working at a major eyeglass chain. He is currently using his paycheck to pay-off the business debts that he personally guaranteed.

The moral of the story is save, save, save and only purchase what you need in the beginning to get up and running. Even if you have saved for your business, it doesn't make sense to spend it all setting up your office. Resist the temptation to make extensive improvements to rental property. You don't get to take the upgrades with you when you leave the rented space. You will need some of those funds for working capital to run the business.

CASE STUDY 22:

Francois had been a hair stylist for ten years, and it had always been his goal to open his own hair salon. He had grandiose plans and wanted to incorporate a book store and a dance studio into his shop. To facilitate this dream, he held a succession of meetings with various friends and business associates to "pick their brains" for free. Initially, many of these people enthusiastically supported him. He was good at what he did, and everyone felt that his salon would be a success.

However, several of his confidants warned him that it appeared he was losing focus on the salon and that a book store in a hair salon could not compete with the larger book retailers and the internet. His proposed location was also questionable because there was no parking lot, and it would be hard for the salon customers to find adequate parking if he was operating three businesses out of one location. His existing hair customers further advised him that a dance studio would be too noisy and that they preferred a serene experience in the salon.

One of his team of free advisors was a CPA. She attended several of his meetings and vigorously warned him against moving so quickly with all of the ventures in one location. She further advised him to consider purchasing, rather than renting, a location since it would require a significant amount of capital to renovate his chosen leased location to accommodate a salon.

Francois did not listen to any of his advisors. He proceeded to sign a ten-year lease on an abandoned building and quickly liquidated all of his savings on improvements to the property. After completing the renovations, he learned that the roof leaked and his lease required that he replace it (another example of why one should get an attorney to review a contract before signing on the dotted line).

By the time Francois finished with the building, he had no funds left to purchase the furniture and fixtures for the salon. He was forced to install only three workstations. Unfortunately, it would

take at least five station renters for him to meet his monthly obliga-
tions. He had also placed his first order of book inventory for the
bookstore but was unable to pay the invoice when it became due.
Therefore, as he sold books, he was unable to restock and was ulti-
mately forced to close the book store. It should be mentioned that no
one ever rented the dance studio because it wasn't soundproof, and
the salon clients complained about the noise.

Francois kept the salon open long enough to find someone
else to take over the lease. He could no longer pay the operating
costs on the large facility. He is now renting a booth in another
salon and is bitter and angry about his business ownership experi-
ence.

Francois had both the talent and the money to open his salon.
However, he made several critical errors in judgment:

- He did not prepare a formal business plan and co-
  located several incompatible businesses.
- He leased a space that was too large and required
  too many improvements on his part to convert to
  a viable hair salon.
- He spent all of his savings too fast on
  the book store and dance studio, and his
  true passion for a hair salon suffered.

Although he continually solicited advice from anyone he
thought could help him, he did not listen to anyone! He acted as
though he knew it all.

Your Financials Shouldn't be an Empty Book

I would be remiss if I failed to briefly explain to you the importance of financial statements (books) to your business. Many small business owners only see their financial statements after their tax preparer has completed their corporate tax returns. At that time they breathe a sigh of relief if they don't owe a lot of money to Uncle Sam, or they blow hot air, blaming their tax preparer if they have to write a big check! They then sign the appropriate paperwork for the return to be e-filed and throw their copy of the tax return in a drawer, never to be seen again.

Your financial statements are more than just information used to prepare your tax returns. They are useful tools in making decisions and evaluating your business, projecting results, and securing financing or funding. Bankers won't even consider you for a business loan if you don't have financial statements.

Your basic financial statements include an income statement, a balance sheet and a statement of cash flow. There are different names for these documents, depending on what industry you are in. However, no matter what they are called, they each tell a story about your business. In my experience, the balance sheet and statement of cash flow are the reports most often ignored by small business owners.

Simply stated, the Balance Sheet shows what you own, who you owe, and what is left over for you, the owner. The Income Statement is a financial statement that most business owners give a little attention. It shows how much money came in (cash basis) or is coming in (accrual basis) versus how much was paid out (cash basis) or is expected to be paid out (accrual basis). Finally, it shows gross profit (the amount of profit on your business operations, excluding selling, general and administrative costs, and interest and taxes) and net income, the final bottom line after all expenses. Cash basis financial statements are exactly what the name implies— financial statements based on the cash that came in and the cash that went out. These statements do not consider what people owe you (accounts receivable) or what you owe others (accounts payable). Accrual basis financial statements take into consideration accounts receivable and accounts payable.

I will not spend any time on the statement of cash flow, except to tell you that it outlines all of the sources and uses of cash in your business.

There is a wealth of knowledge that can be gleaned from your financial statements if they are setup correctly to capture the information you need for decision making. When I set up a client's financial statements, I prefer to err on the side of too much detail. It's easier to cease providing certain data than it is to go back and capture that data later. As a small business, some of the information that will be useful to you includes:

- Comparative financial statements to show trends. The trends that you see when reviewing these statements can help you answer questions such as:
  - Did your business generate more revenues this year/month than the previous year/ month?
  - Have there been unanticipated increases in certain expense categories?
  - Were the increases proportionate with the increase in revenues?

- Ratio Analysis to show how you compare with others in your industry, how you compare with your own historical results, and help you answer key business performance questions such as:
  - Have you taken on too much debt or can you handle more debt?
  - Are your customers paying you more slowly than in the past?
  - Are you colleting your receivables in a timely manner?
  - Are you maintaining too much or too little inventory?
- Budget versus Actual reports to get a handle on your spending relative to your budget. Keep in mind that if you are growing, your budget may need to be updated frequently.
- Reports by product, business segment, funding source, etc. to help show you where you are making money and where you may need to make adjustments
- Cash flow projections to tell you when you can expect to receive cash, who you owe, and when you have to pay them, and if you will have enough cash on hand to pay them.

It is important that you let your accountant know what information you want to know about your business on a regular basis so he or she can set up your financial statements accordingly. And don't just toss your financial statements in a file cabinet. Read them, question them, use them to find ways to improve and grow your business.

©timtim.com

"Don't wait until everything is just right. It will never be perfect. There will always be challenges, obstacles and less than perfect conditions. So what. Get started now. With each step you take, you will grow stronger and stronger, more and more skilled, more and more self-confident and more and more successful."

--Mark Victor Hansen,
Motivational speaker, trainer and author

Say Goodbye to the Basement

Many successful entrepreneurs launched their businesses in their home office, garage or basement (à la Robert T. Kiyosaki, author of Rich Dad, Poor Dad, and Steve Jobs of Apple). But as the business grew, they moved on to rent office space outside of the home. However, those who lacked financial discipline often found themselves back in the basement several years later. Build your business correctly so you can say goodbye to the basement forever!

You now have an idea of some of the things you need to do to get your business started and ensure that you are less likely to be "here today and gone tomorrow." Your startup business plan is complete, and you are prepared to move forward. You have read 'The Naked Truth of Owning a Business' (final shameless plug) and have concluded that the lifestyle of a business owner is for you!

Keep the following points in mind as you enter your Land of Oz:

- Incorporate your business if necessary! Hire an attorney or CPA experienced with business structures. Make sure you have done your homework.
- Open a business bank account to ensure that your personal and business transactions are clearly separate.

- If you think you want a business partner, make sure you hire an experienced attorney to prepare any agreements you need to outline how your partnership will operate. Remember to include an exit strategy. Also, be sure to research the person you'll be getting into the business marriage bed with (background checks, credit reports, etc. are good tools for gauging a person's spending and paying habits).

- Make sure your business plans include technology. In some industries, current technology is necessary to compete effectively.

- Remember that your business plan is a dynamic document that will change as your business transforms and grows. Review it and make sure that your assumptions are still valid.

- Don't try to be your own attorney, CPA, or technology consultant. Search out professionals who are willing to work with you as your business grows. For many of my smaller customers, I charge a fee that is manageable to them in the earlier years, with the understanding that my rates will increase as their business grows and my responsibilities increase.

- File and pay your taxes in a timely manner.

- Make sure any family members that you hire are qualified to perform the job. Screen them like you would any other candidate. If you decide to hire an unqualified family member for the sake of the family then don't force other professionals to report to them.

- Listen to the professionals you hire. Other business owners may have received different advice than you have about certain subjects. There may be good reasons why. Listen to the professionals you hire, and if they can't explain their recommendations to you in a manner that you understand, hire new ones.
- Listen to your employees.
- Remember that cash flow is critical to small businesses. Update your personal and business budgets and maintain financial discipline.
- Review your financial statements and use them as a tool to manage your business. Don't just throw them in a drawer.

Now that you have the information, courage, and determination to travel that entrepreneural yellow brick road...go ahead and live your dreams!!!

APPENDIX (AKA: The Boring Stuff)

BUSINESS STRUCTURES

Sole Proprietor: A sole proprietorship is the simplest form of business. In a nutshell, it is when someone owns an unincorporated business by himself or herself. Sole proprietors are not required to file separate income tax returns for the business because the business income and expenses are reported on their personal income tax returns. If you opt for this structure, you should be fairly certain that personal liability won't be a problem and that you will have adequate business insurance.

Keep in mind that just because you elect to be a sole proprietor does not mean that you can have a free for all with your books and records. You should still maintain accurate records and documentation of business transactions, or the IRS could come swinging your way...and trust me, they don't miss.

S Corporations: S Corporations are domestic corporations that have no more than 100 shareholders and one class of stock. The shareholders can be individuals, certain trusts, and estates. However, Partnerships, Corporations and non-resident aliens cannot be shareholders. Although separate business tax returns must be filed for S Corporations, shareholders report the flow-through of income and losses on their personal tax returns and are assessed tax at their individual income tax rates. This allows S Corporations to avoid double taxation on the corporate income. (Stop yawning! I am moving along as quickly as I can.)

Partnerships: A Partnership is when two or more people join together in matrimony (just kidding, but it's almost the same). It's when they join to carry on a trade or business, and each person (hopefully) contributes something to the Partnership (money, property, labor, expertise or just plain old common sense) and expects to share in the profits and losses of the business.

A Partnership files an annual information return to report the income, deductions, gains, losses, etc., from its operations, but it does not pay income tax. Instead, it "passes through" any profits or losses to its partners. Each partner is required to include his or her share of the Partnership's income or loss on his or her personal tax return. Partners are not employees and are not issued a Form W-2. The Partnership must furnish copies of the K-1 to the partners for use in preparing their personal income tax returns.

Limited Liability Companies: A Limited Liability Company (LLC) is a business structure governed by state statute, which means that the rules, requirements, etc. will vary by state. LLCs are popular because, like Corporations, owners have limited personal liability for the debts and actions of the LLC. However, other features of LLCs are more like a Partnership, providing management flexibility and the benefit of pass-through taxation. Owners of an LLC are called members, and there is generally no maximum or minimum number of members. The federal government does not recognize an LLC as a classification for federal tax purposes. An LLC business entity files a Corporation, Partnership or Sole Proprietorship tax return.

Only one more to go…stay with me.

Corporations: A Corporation is a legal entity with limited liability, centralization of management, perpetual duration and ease of transferability of ownership interests. The owners of a Corporation are called "shareholders." Corporations file federal and state tax returns with no pass through to their shareholders. They pay their own income taxes and can elect to pay dividends to the shareholders.

Whew! That was a mouthful, but being familiar with the distinctions between the business structures is important. There are other, more complex, structures that your attorney may recommend but the basics are outlined above.

EMPLOYMENT TAXES

Social Security Taxes: As an employer, you are responsible for withholding social security taxes from employees' paychecks and remitting them to the government. You are also responsible for matching the amount you withhold from your employees and paying into social security on their behalf. In the past, the employer paid the same percentage on behalf of the employee as was withheld from the employee. However, in recent years the amounts have differed due to tax holidays and hiring-stimulus plans enacted by Congress. In 2011, the employer paid 6.2% of the employees wage base as social security taxes, while only 4.2% was withheld from the employee.

Social security taxes are paid on only a portion of an employee's wages, referred to as the wage base. In 2011 the social security tax base was $106,400 of an employee's wages. In 2012, the social security wage base increased to $110,100. This cap has been hotly debated in Congress and the press in recent years. Some believe that it is unfair to subject the entire salary of low-wage earners to social security taxes but only the first hundred thousand dollars or so of the salary of the highly compensated. I suspect this issue will be debated for many years before any significant changes are made. Just know that social security taxes will be one of your larger tax burdens.

Medicare Taxes: The ability to participate in the Medicare program is not a gift that the federal government gives to us as some suggest. We pay for it through the Medicare tax. Much like social security taxes, the employer is required to withhold Medicare taxes from an employee's paycheck and match that amount. All of an employee's earnings are subject to the Medicare tax rate of 1.45%.

Unemployment Taxes: State unemployment taxes are entirely an employer burden; nothing is withheld from your employees' paychecks for this tax. The percent and wage base will vary from state to state and from company to company.

Finally, as an employer, you are required to pay into the federal unemployment tax fund. For 2012, the tax rate is 6.0% and applies only to the first $7,000 in wages you pay to each employee. Generally, you can take a credit against your federal unemployment taxes for amounts you paid into state unemployment funds.

A must-have for anyone who is *thinking* about starting a business!

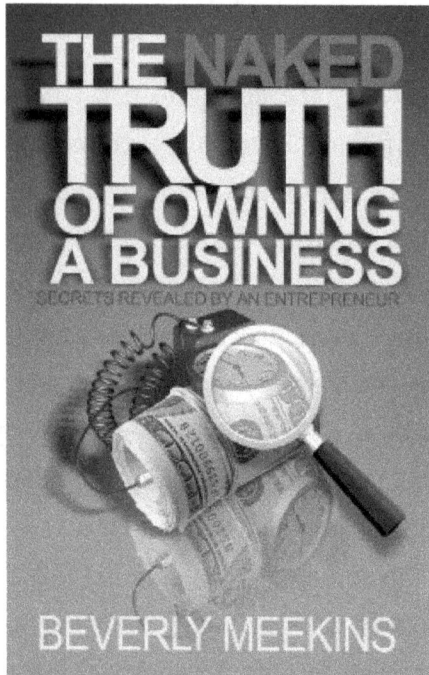

Business owners enthusiastically proclaim the joys of business ownership; however, most have not always shared the naked truth about the flipside. There's a whole lot more to launching and sustaining a successful business than just choosing a name, an organization structure, and raking in the dough.

In her first book, Beverly Meekins, a CPA and entrepreneur with over twenty years in the industry, discusses what many successful business owners learned the hard way and reveals secrets that everyone should know before embarking on the entrepreneur's yellow brick road.

Certified Life Coach, Empowerment Coach, Intuitive Counselor,
Author and Motivational Speaker

Ever wondered why you are stuck at the same point in your
life? Do you ponder how you can enhance your life, your
career, and your relationships? Ehryck F. Gilmore, CH points
you to answers to these questions and more …

Coming soon...

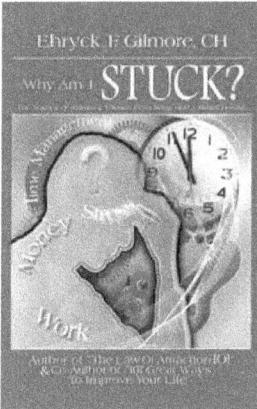

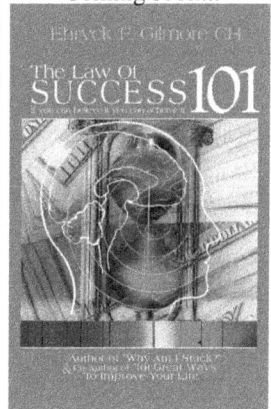

Newsweek explores the
secrets behind "THE SECRET"

Journalist and photographers, from
Newsweek paid Ehryck F. Gilmore
a visit at his Chicago home to tap
into his thoughts on this new, but
not quite new, phenomenon,
The Law Of Attraction.
Visit Ehryck's website to check out
the article.

www.ehryckgilmore.com

About the Author

Beverly has worked in many business and financial disciplines for more than twenty years. She lives in the suburbs of Chicago with her husband and two dogs, Bailey and Blade. She is a certified public accountant and certified internal auditor, with an accounting degree from the University of Illinois and a Master of Business Administration from the University of Chicago. She owns The Meekins Group, a CPA and business consulting firm located in the suburbs of Chicago, Illinois (www.themeekinsgroup.com). Her first book in the Naked Truth series is entitled The Naked Truth of Owning a Business – Secrets Revealed by an Entrepreneur. This is the second book in the series.

Visit www.bampublishingco.com to learn more about her current and upcoming projects.

www.ingramcontent.com/pod-product-compliance
Lightning Source LLC
LaVergne TN
LVHW091155080426
835509LV00006B/704